*The Oculatum*

# THE *Oculatum*

A BOOK OF GREAT INSIGHT
FOR THOSE WHO WISH TO SEE

Butler Yates

DUTTON

DUTTON
Published by the Penguin Group
Penguin Putnam Inc., 375 Hudson Street,
New York, New York 10014, U.S.A.
Penguin Books Ltd, 80 Strand, London WC2R 0RL, England
Penguin Books Australia Ltd, 250 Camberwell Road,
Camberwell, Victoria 3124, Australia
Penguin Books Canada Ltd, 10 Alcorn Avenue, Toronto, Ontario, Canada M4V 3B2
Penguin Books (N.Z.) Ltd, Cnr Rosedale and Airborne Roads, Albany, Auckland
1310, New Zealand

Penguin Books Ltd, Registered Offices: Harmondsworth, Middlesex, England

Published by Dutton, a member of Penguin Putnam Inc.

First printing, February 2003
1 3 5 7 9 10 8 6 4 2



LIBRARY OF CONGRESS CATALOGING-IN-PUBLICATION DATA

Yates, Butler.
The Oculatum : a book of great insight for those who wish to see / by Butler Yates.
p. cm.
ISBN 0-525-94717-5 (alk. paper)
1. Choice (Psychology)—Quotations, maxims, etc. I. Title.

BF611 .Y38 2003
133.3—dc21
2002073953

Printed in the United States of America
Set in Nicholas Cochin
Designed by Jaye Zimet



This book is printed on acid-free paper. ∞

For
Don Browning

With much appreciation to all who have made this endeavor possible. In Europe, Messrs. Harry Maynard and Maurice Libby. In Arkansas, Ms. Wilma Lewis and Mr. Gary Miller. My agent Ms. Neeti Madan and her assistant Ms. Sarah Walsh, of Sterling Lord Literistic. My editor Ms. Laurie Chittenden and her assistant Ms. Stephanie Bowe, of Penguin Putnam. I am exceedingly grateful to Mr. Mark F. Hampton, of Hampton Larkowski, P.A., of Little Rock, for his unflagging support, encouragement, and good counsel.

Butler Yates

# *The Oculatum*

A BOOK OF GREAT INSIGHT
FOR THOSE WHO WISH TO SEE

The everyday word we use to define protection from future illness or potential calamity, the word we use to describe our most precious organ of sight, and the word we use to denote new life in nature all share a common bond. These three words—inoculate, eye, and bud—though seemingly most diverse, are formed from the very same Latin root: *oculus*. It may therefore not be coincidental that a medieval manuscript offering great solace, perception, and guidance should have been entitled *The Oculatum*.

SUGGESTED INSTRUCTIONS

You shall *"spake time six these words, three times"* at *"matins, lauds and at vespers"* and do this *"six full days"* and then *"take rest,"* explained the instructions to the original *Oculatum*. In this present rendition, as with the original, the reader must make several choices. *The Oculatum* may offer clarity, strength, and awareness for the attentive reader in his or her daily life. It has no beginning, no end, and may be read in either direction. First, the reader may choose which cover to open, for the book opens both ways. That choice being made, the reader may decide which is the top and bottom of the page, for both are correct, and then may choose to begin. Being now at the beginning of a section, it is suggested that the four-line phrase that comes to view be read six times, silently or in voice. Repeat this action three times during the day, perhaps on waking, at a mid-point, and upon retiring. The following day the process is repeated for the next page and so on for a six-day period. It is of no consequence for the reader to remember, understand, or comprehend the phrase; it matters only that it be read. For it should be upon the completion of the sixth day that the reader may discover a greater sense of focus and awareness. Any decisions to be made can now be acted upon. If the reader desires, the process may be repeated in the same section or in any other as described above.

# *The Oculatum*

## A BRIEF HISTORY

In September 1666 the city of London was ravaged by a great fire. Some four hundred fifty acres were burnt bare, sixty-nine churches were destroyed, and ten souls were known to have perished. The inferno blazed for more than four days, and the citizens could only watch their metropolis turn to ash. To the east of the city, at the Friary on Blackheath, among those seeking sanctuary from the flames was a family most familiar with life's hardship, but more familiar with life's hope. Their leader was a man of Flemish descent named Joseph Van dar Lippen. Some ninety years before, his great-great grandfather had led a similar group to safety in England from the fires of persecution in Europe. Van dar Lippen kept about him a memento of his forebear and referred to it often as it always gave strength, hope, and comfort. Van dar Lippen's memento was a *"smallest book or folio"* that *"would allow several ways of reading."* Made of *"loose papers"* it *"let there be changing of their order."* It contained *"many writings"* and was *"rough and used much."* There was *"much good thought"* and *"wisdom within."* It was *The Oculatum*. Originally passed down by word of mouth, *The Oculatum* became a collection of wisdom that might be read in time of need. With the invention of the printing press, similar wise sayings would spread through Europe in a flood of pamphlets and almanacs.

I came across mention of *The Oculatum* while researching bricks—another story altogether. The medieval era was marked by great superstition. To ensure safety and harmony, masons would hide scraps of paper containing wisdom and well-wishes between the bricks. These phrases were the basis for the original *Oculatum*. Later, they were collected and I chanced upon newspapers, almanacs, and psalters in London, Antwerp, and Venice containing this wisdom.

# *The Oculatum*

Chance
and
certainty
are one

---

Hold firm
the tiding
of pure
example

Courage
creates
change
within

---

A wise man
will plan
of winter
in the spring

Read well
your enemy
and you
will learn

---

Temptation
of haste
brings forth
slow regret

Fight not
against
the tempest
flow in it

---

Be not
in slumber
as the light
shines out

The lust
of power
grows in
weakness

---

Patience
and time
win out
the tempest

Blame others
and you
curse
yourself

---

With not
tempest
there is
not calm

Hear not
the answer
but
the question

---

The voyage
is soon forgot
when landfall
comes to sight

We will
not forget
our
falsehoods

---

The voyage
is not hard
'tis the
setting sail

Truth
needs
not
memory

---

Close keep
a friend
closer keep
your foe

Our
secrets
blackmail
the soul

---

Good chance
knows well
who soon
prepare

In the
stillness
the soul
will speak

---

Hurry not
the morrow
save you
lose the day

For all
there is
but one
voyage

---

Hunt
two rabbits
bag neither
one

Choose
your
family
well

---

Believe not
beauty true
nor that
ugly false

Strive to
be heroic
without
notice

---

Beware
a wise man
who knows
he is wise

Fear is
conquered
with
faith

Your enemy
is friend
not yet
known

Growth
is easier
without
resistance

---

Ridicule
the pauper
be made
poorer also

Our eyes
blind first
in our
heart

---

The smooth
road
makes dull
the journey

Simple
is
the
spirit

---

Eloquent talk
may not
speak sure
the truth

There is
not anger
in
acceptance

---

Trick
not oneself
to seduce
another

The crop
needs every
season to
grow strong

---

Speak not
the words
you would
not follow

To journey
you must
first
go out

---

Forgive
your enemy
but so too
your friend

The victor
may not win
but will
take part

---

Gain
most
by
giving

The empty
word needs
the louder
sound

---

We did not
ask for life
do not ask
to live

We came
with nothing
and will take
the same

---

Be always
hero
to the
children

We are
not one nor
the other
but all

---

Search
not for
superstition
over truth

Foe or friend
are the
same
without us

---

Mighty
is the man
who stands
alone

Remember
we are
children
*still*

---

Start
much
finish
little

Know well
that you
may not
know

---

The best
revenge
is complete
forgiveness

Fear
shall be
cleansed
in honesty

---

Bequeath
the gift
of good
example

Thought
precedes action
that precedes
consequence

---

Do no thing
by half
best wrong
than ill tried

?

¿

Life is full
of choice
we dare
not to see

---

A white lie
will turn
coal black
in telling

You have
all that
you shall
ever need

---

The grand
thought
does justify
a sinful act

Seek
for purpose
more
than pride

---

Courtesy
cost nought
yet shall
purchase all

Feed the
soul for
you will
not starve

---

Cast out
resentment
for it feeds
upon itself

Fear
not death
fear
not life

---

Appetite
comes
with
eating

Change
will
be not
shackled

---

Sweep
your own
house
first

?

¿

Pray you
will find
not that
you seek

---

A good anvil
shall not
fear
the hammer

Loving
and forgiving
are true
intertwined

---

The truest
enjoyment
be not found
but earned

The greatest
of conflict
shall be
within

---

The guilty
heart
needs no
accuser

No labor
shall be
without
grace

---

Esteem
is easier
made than
recovered

Be of
patience
about
oneself

---

A wise man
knows well
his lack
of knowing

Accept
our fault
so too
our virtue

---

Good habits
grow of
temptations
denied

?

¿

Pleasure
shall be
in all
things

---

Sinfulness
and folly
have long
memory

Life
is more
precious
in death

---

Grow
happiness
where you
stand

Plan not
the future
within
the past

---

Be thankful
of hardship
not that
of others

Our very
will may
avail us
little

---

A pleasure
shared
is twice
multiplied

The answer
lays bound
within
the question

---

If you fail
to learn
you so fail
to teach

Repair
wrongs
with
haste

---

Gratitude
should
be not
silent

Follow
no one
you would
not lead

---

The wise man
considers all
but may
little accept

That given
in grace
shall be
returned over

---

The folly
not repaired
is often
repeated

Our most
constant
companion
is change

---

A neighbor's
misfortune
is ours
also

We may not
impart
that we
do not hold

---

A love word
shall warm
a winter
of loathing

Truth
speaks
but few
words

---

Give
not advice
give only
example

Your
own words
may strike
you deaf

---

Ignorance
is the
great
fearmonger

?

¿

The noble
require
not
recognition

---

We are
most gullible
to our own
untruth

Charity
needs
not
motive

---

Our
strength
is equal to
our burden

Not two
things are like
yet each relies
the other

---

Knowledge
is often
a choice
by wisdom

Flattery
shall turn
reason
dull

---

Most
strident
are the
uncertain

View not
the trifles
without
the whole

---

Doubt
first
then
learn

With
acceptance
there is
change

---

No fiend
constant
more than
temptation

One
may make
a path
for many

---

Do not
cut
that you
may unite

To change
fortune
change
within

---

Loan no coin
to friend
save you
lose both

We begin
on fresh
each every
day

---

Destiny
awaits
at every
turning

Tragedy
is the
greatest
teacher

---

What a fool
does last
a wise man
does first

To learn
we should
forget not
the past

---

Down no man's
faith
that your own
is better

Speak but
the tongue
of good
example

---

Be no beggar
to the morrow
if your purse
is bare today

The pure
voice
need not
whisper

---

We are
known
by our
fellows

The joy
not shared
with others
withers soon

---

Fortune
is often
in company
of effort

Forget not
tragedy
for it will
strengthen

---

Truth
shall
fear not
question

Smooth sea
made not
the hero
captain

---

Trust
not
till
proved

Speak words
first upon
the heart
then mouth

---

Our most
devious foe
slumbers
within

Small effort
is required
for great
dishonor

---

The laborer
will easy see
the baker's
daily toil

Seek good
for it
may then
find you

---

In envy
there is
nought
enjoying

Judge not
your fellow
lest you
be judged

---

Beware
the man
of one
sure mind

We are soon
defeated
by our own
quick hand

---

The flower
of friend
has not
thorn

Barren winter
brings forth
the fruitful
spring

---

That we
may fail
should not
deter us

The heart
of faith
fears not
of man

---

To win
small note
we may lose
all respect

Any path
will lead
with not
direction

---

Not
try
not
fail

Our trifle
wants
do soon
enslave us

---

Pity
the debtor
above
the pauper

Nought
will come
to the
closed door

---

There is no
good cause
for anger
to another

The
impossible
was once
a dream

---

Be honest
to yourself
be honest
to another

This day

will not

soon

return

---

Want not

justice

ask only

mercy

In virtue
there is
always
reward

---

Be not fool
on first look
for show is
no substance

See not
your fate
in others
faces

---

Lock not
for that
you have
no key

Triumph
is born
out of
adversity

---

Do not
hasty knot
that you may
not untie

For in everything there is choice

---

Not of man is so perfect that can not be improved

Not but
misfortunes
grow of
your garden

---

The sinful
choose not sin
they know not
happiness

Seek
anew
for it
is there

---

Choose
not decide
a choice
you make

The loving
spirit
is not
defeated

---

To decide
is not
to act
but prepare

Obtain
with love
that refused
in force

---

Would
the eagle
know he flies
so high

Let no
man
think
for you

---

A great city
is built
up from
single stones

Be not
what
you
are not

---

Savor
each
day
slowly

To give love
we must
love first
ourself

A mountain
is made of
small stones
drawn close

Courage
shows not
by dying
but living

---

Seek out
the faultless
and you will
end alone

Well listen
to that
you do not
wish to hear

---

A true word
shall not
harm
the speaker

From
dark night
comes
dawn light

---

The evil lie
is the
word
not spoke

Holding
to the past
will deny
the present

---

Give honest
effort
into
every task

In age
keep but
the faith
of babes

---

A great sin
is to be
aware
of none

Our tears
will wash
both sorrow
and gladness

---

Rough sea
will aid
the able
captain

Remember
first others
forget
last yourself

---

'Tis but
another plate
will satisfy
the glutton

All
truth
is most
loving

---

Humility
is observed
when not
displayed

False
humility
is of
conceit

---

Have but
around you
all you see
beautiful

We may
not avoid
our
destiny

---

Ask not
your fellow
that you
can do

Only
the good
feel
guilt

---

Steal
knowledge
from each
you meet

Stronger
to *sway*
of the storm
than sever

---

Promise made
in the storm
is forgotten
in the calm

Ask of
the traveled
to know well
the voyage

---

Better to
light a lamp
than stumble
in the dark

Listen
well
for you
may hear

---

Wisdom
is born
from
wonder

Honor
has the
keenest
sight

---

A clean hand
needs
not
washing

Embrace
the past
but live
not there

---

A wise man
will change
his view
a fool never

All

is in

perfect

order

---

The hungry

will not

complain

the meal

To be gentle
shows the
greatest
of strength

---

Ford
the stream
where it is
shallow

This
season
will also
change

---

Rather
to repair
than to
apologize

Uncover
who you
are and
rejoice

---

Nothing
is new
but change
of old

Life
is love
and love
is giving

---

As you
do more
you will
do more

False beauty
has no
enemy
save time

---

Also
the lion
suffers
flies

Trust only
in the
proof
of action

---

In all things
a little
is enough
to suffice

An
open door
allows in
the light

---

The jewel
*sparkles* not
without
burnish

Life
is our
great gift
well use it

---

'T is not
coincidence
two ears
one tongue

To influence
your enemy
first listen
of him

---

Listen
first
then
hear

Hide not
the past
nor
live there

---

Stones
build walls
but so to
bridges

Everything
we have
has
been given

---

Live
in private
as in
public

We
do
nothing
alone

---

Our fall
from grace
comes on
in long days

The spirit
the body
the mind
are one

---

Praising
words
wither
quickly

Words
of honor
do not
scar

---

Desperate
needs
bring odd
bedfellows

Hear
your
own
words

---

Abundance
brings forth
our will
to squander

Consequence
brings
great
learning

---

Stride out
to leave
footsteps
of your own

Respect well
the right
of your
rival

---

The silver
tongue may
often talk
in tarnish

Know
first
your
path

---

Many are
our gifts
we do
not use

Add only
sweet song
to the
silence

---

Better
a friend true
than many
false fawners

From
within
the light
shines

---

Plant seed
before
you plan
the harvest

Know well
yourself
and be
of thanks

---

Discard
not the old
till the new
is proved

Be not
friend
to false
expectation

---

A poacher's
bag
is never
full

Blessed
are those
who need
not blame

---

The egg
must break
for the eagle
to fly

Have
strength
enough to
seek help

---

Complacence
be friend
of certain
failure

All life
is an
unimagined
gift

---

To wait
is often
the bolder
action

In every
chaos
there is
order

---

That despised
of others
we soon see
of our self

There
is not
worry
in faith

---

Fear not to
grow olden
better fear
not to grow

You are in
all things
if you
will it

---

The wise
journeyman
will measure
twice fold

Return
always
to your
heart

---

Look to
the light
and shadows
fall behind

Pity
and pray
for the
powermonger

---

Claim not
as right
that given
in gift

Forget
not
who
you are

---

Progress
comes not
without
change

With all
judgment
there is
fear

---

'Tis better
travel alone
than join with
rogues' company

Misfortune
will
follow
the fool

---

The mummer
has often
the clearest
of voice

Risk nothing
and that
shall be
your reward

---

Every voyage
has both
the tempest
and the calm

*The Oculatum*

"*loose papers*" it "*let there be changing of their order.*" It contained "*many writings*" and was "*rough and used much.*" There was "*much good thought*" and "*wisdom within.*" It was *The Oculatum*. Originally passed down by word of mouth, *The Oculatum* became a collection of wisdom that might be read in time of need. With the invention of the printing press, similar wise sayings would spread through Europe in a flood of pamphlets and almanacs.

I came across mention of *The Oculatum* while researching bricks—another story altogether. The medieval era was marked by great superstition. To ensure safety and harmony, masons would hide scraps of paper containing wisdom and well-wishes between the bricks. These phrases were the basis for the original *Oculatum*. Later, they were collected and I chanced upon newspapers, almanacs, and psalters in London, Antwerp, and Venice containing this wisdom.

# *The Oculatum*

## A BRIEF HISTORY

In September 1666 the city of London was ravaged by a great fire. Some four hundred fifty acres were burnt bare, sixty-nine churches were destroyed, and ten souls were known to have perished. The inferno blazed for more than four days, and the citizens could only watch their metropolis turn to ash. To the east of the city, at the Friary on Blackheath, among those seeking sanctuary from the flames was a family most familiar with life's hardship, but more familiar with life's hope. Their leader was a man of Flemish descent named Joseph Van dar Lippen. Some ninety years before, his great-great grandfather had led a similar group to safety in England from the fires of persecution in Europe. Van dar Lippen kept about him a memento of his forebear and referred to it often as it always gave strength, hope, and comfort. Van dar Lippen's memento was a "*smallest book or folio*" that "*would allow several ways of reading.*" Made of attentive reader in his or her daily life. It has no beginning, no end, and may be read in either direction. First, the reader may choose which cover to open, for the book opens both ways. That choice being made, the reader may decide which is the top and bottom of the page, for both are correct, and then may choose to begin. Being now at the beginning of a section, it is suggested that the four-line phrase that comes to view be read six times, silently or in voice. Repeat this action three times during the day, perhaps on waking, at a mid-point, and upon retiring. The following day the process is repeated for the next page and so on for a six-day period. It is of no consequence for the reader to remember, understand, or comprehend the phrase; it matters only that it be read. For it should be upon the completion of the sixth day that the reader may discover a greater sense of focus and awareness. Any decisions to be made can now be acted upon. If the reader desires, the process may be repeated in the same section or in any other as described above.

# *The Oculatum*

A BOOK OF GREAT INSIGHT
FOR THOSE WHO WISH TO SEE

The everyday word we use to define protection from future illness or potential calamity, the word we use to describe our most precious organ of sight, and the word we use to denote new life in nature all share a common bond. These three words—inoculate, eye, and bud—though seemingly most diverse, are formed from the very same Latin root: *oculus*. It may therefore not be coincidental that a medieval manuscript offering great solace, perception, and guidance should have been entitled *The Oculatum*.

SUGGESTED INSTRUCTIONS

You shall *"spake time six these words, three times"* at *"matins, lauds and at vespers"* and do this *"six full days"* and then *"take rest,"* explained the instructions to the original *Oculatum*. In this present rendition, as with the original, the reader must make several choices. *The Oculatum* may offer clarity, strength, and awareness for the

With much appreciation to all who have made this endeavor possible. In Europe, Messrs. Harry Maynard and Maurice Libby. In Arkansas, Ms. Wilma Lewis and Mr. Gary Miller. My agent Ms. Neeti Madan and her assistant Ms. Sarah Walsh, of Sterling Lord Literistic. My editor Ms. Laurie Chittenden and her assistant Ms. Stephanie Bowe, of Penguin Putnam. I am exceedingly grateful to Mr. Mark F. Hampton, of Hampton Larkowski, P.A., of Little Rock, for his unflagging support, encouragement, and good counsel.

Butler Yates

For

Don Browning

# THE *Oculatum*

A BOOK OF GREAT INSIGHT
FOR THOSE WHO WISH TO SEE

Butler Yates

DUTTON

*The Oculatum*